# HOMESTEADING

## SETTLING AMERICA'S HEARTLAND

DOROTHY HINSHAW PATENT

PHOTOGRAPHS BY WILLIAM MUÑOZ

Walker and Company  New York

*For those who still share the pioneering spirit*

# Acknowledgments

The author and photographer wish to thank Jan Charlo, Marsha Dunn, Joanne Farley, H. Corwin Hinshaw, Sandy and Sean Muñoz, Bill and Wanda Schnider, Laura Van Horn, the Denver Public Library, Homestead National Monument, Nebraska State Historical Society, Prairie Homestead, Sod House Museum, Valley View School, and the Wilder Homestead for their help with this book.

First published in the United States of America in 1998 by Walker Publishing Company, Inc.

Published simultaneously in Canada by Thomas Allen & Son Canada, Limited, Markham, Ontario.

Library of Congress Cataloging-in-Publication Data
Patent, Dorothy Hinshaw.
Homesteading: settling America's heartland/Dorothy Hinshaw Patent; photographs by William Muñoz.
        p. cm.
Summary: Chronicles the activities of the homesteaders who settled the vast American prairies during the late nineteenth and early twentieth centuries.
ISBN 0-8027-8664-2 (hardcover). —ISBN 0-8027-8665-0 (reinforced)
1. Frontier and pioneer life—West (U.S.)—Juvenile literature.
2. West (U.S.)—Social life and customs—Juvenile literature.
[1. Frontier and pioneer life—West (U.S.) 2. West (U.S.)—Social life and customs.]
I. Muñoz, William, ill. II. Title.
        F596.P38 1998
        978—dc21                                                                      98-12463
                                                                                              CIP
                                                                                              AC

BOOK DESIGN BY DIANE HOBBING OF SNAP-HAUS GRAPHICS

Printed in Hong Kong

10 9 8 7 6 5 4 3 2 1

**E**very morning Wanda Schnider slips out from under her warm quilt before dawn and builds a fire in the wood stove that provides the only heat for her home. Then she puts the wash in the bathtub and heads for the kitchen to prepare breakfast. She grinds some wheat using a hand grinder and mixes up the pancake batter. By eight o'clock, she's eaten breakfast with her

*Like homesteading women, Wanda Schnider grinds wheat to bake bread for her family.*

3

*Wanda chops wood for the stove that heats the home and cooks the food.*

husband, Bill, gotten homemade bread under way, cleaned up the kitchen, and done the laundry by hand—all in the log home she and Bill built from timber that Bill cut.

Wanda and Bill live today much like the homesteaders who settled the vast American prairies during the late nineteenth and early twentieth centuries. Long days and hard work make up their lives, as was true for the homesteaders. But Wanda and Bill have a choice to do things the old way. The homesteaders had no such choices. They had to work hard, doing everything for themselves, or they could lose their land or even starve in a harsh winter.

When the Homestead Act was passed in 1862, the United States was a rapidly changing country. The Civil War had begun in the South, the cities of the Northeast were growing, and peak settlement of the Far West along the Oregon Trail had passed. America was experiencing growing pains, among which were its relations with American Indians who lived on the vast prairies that separated the eastern states from the faraway Pacific Coast. Fear on both sides sometimes led to mistrust and violence. Ultimately, American Indians lost their land, and an American way of life ended as they were moved to reservations.

This book focuses not on an era in American history but rather on a specific group of people who lived within it—the homesteaders. Their personal struggles and victories helped shape the United States as we know it. This is their story—how they came to the land of promise and what they had to do to survive once they arrived there.

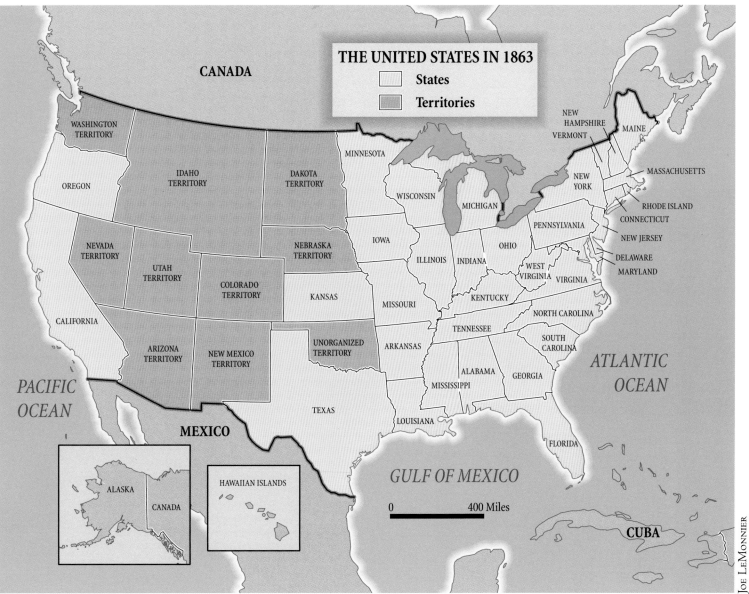

THE UNITED STATES IN 1863
States
Territories

CANADA

WASHINGTON TERRITORY

OREGON

IDAHO TERRITORY

DAKOTA TERRITORY

MINNESOTA

NEW HAMPSHIRE
VERMONT
MAINE

MASSACHUSETTS

NEVADA TERRITORY

UTAH TERRITORY

COLORADO TERRITORY

NEBRASKA TERRITORY

WISCONSIN

MICHIGAN

NEW YORK

RHODE ISLAND
CONNECTICUT

IOWA

PENNSYLVANIA

NEW JERSEY

ILLINOIS

INDIANA

OHIO

DELAWARE
MARYLAND

CALIFORNIA

KANSAS

MISSOURI

WEST VIRGINIA

VIRGINIA

ARIZONA TERRITORY

NEW MEXICO TERRITORY

UNORGANIZED TERRITORY

ARKANSAS

TENNESSEE

KENTUCKY

NORTH CAROLINA

SOUTH CAROLINA

PACIFIC OCEAN

TEXAS

MISSISSIPPI

ALABAMA

GEORGIA

ATLANTIC OCEAN

LOUISIANA

MEXICO

FLORIDA

GULF OF MEXICO

ALASKA
CANADA

HAWAIIAN ISLANDS

0    400 Miles

CUBA

JOE LEMONNIER

5

# Filling the Empty Land

*T*he first pioneers to go west ignored the land later settled by homesteaders. During the mid-1800s travelers hurried across the prairies, eager to reach the rich farmlands and goldfields of what are now the states of California, Oregon, and Washington. Even children's schoolbooks called the prairie the "Great American Desert" because many saw the land as vast and useless as a desert. A few heading west saw the potential for growing crops on these rolling, almost treeless grasslands, but settlement there was not allowed. Treaties had set the land aside for American Indians.

In the early 1860s politicians began to worry about the empty prairie. How could they govern a divided country when even transporting goods from one part to the other and keeping up communication between the two coasts was so difficult? The government in those days didn't think of American Indians as potential citizens, and they decided the prairies needed to be settled by people of European origin. Treaties with the Indians were broken, and eventually they were driven out and forced to settle in other areas.

In 1862 Congress passed the Homestead Act, and President Abraham Lincoln signed it. "This will do something for the little fellow," he is said to have commented. The act was effective as of January 1, 1863. Galusha Grow, the Pennsylvania representative

*Many homesteaders arrived in covered wagons. Today some people enjoy reliving the covered-wagon experience on weekend trips (facing page).*

*This document is the patent granting Daniel Freeman ownership of the land he claimed in 1863.*

*To some, the promise of agricultural riches on the treeless prairie was more valuable than dreams of gold in the West.*

who authored the act, called it "free land for free men." The act allowed any citizen (or person who had declared his or her intention to become a citizen) who was the head of a household to lay claim to 160 acres of public land. That's a piece of land a half-mile long and a half-mile wide. He or she had to be at least twenty-one years old and pay just $18—a $14 filing fee and another $4 five years later. Eighteen dollars could buy a lot more then than it can now, but it was still a bargain for a family farm in the 1800s.

To become the owner of the land, the homesteader had to dig a well and build a house. He or she also had to plow at least twenty acres to grow crops and had to put in fences. With modern equipment, twenty acres can easily be plowed in a few hours. But breaking up twenty acres of prairie sod back then, using horses or oxen,

*This land was plowed by a machine. With only oxen or horses for help, a homesteader could work from dawn to dusk and have just a small area ready for crops.*

*This homestead house stands on the land of Daniel Freeman, one of the first homesteaders to claim land on the first day possible, January 1, 1863. His homestead was on very good land that featured a stream and trees.*

meant many days of backbreaking labor. Harvesting grain was even more difficult. To harvest an acre of wheat and prepare it for market took three days. A modern machine can do the work in six minutes!

After five years of living on the land and successfully developing it as a farm, the homesteader could file for his patent on the property, which gave him full ownership. This process was called "proving up." From then on the farm belonged to him, just as if he had bought and paid for it.

With the Homestead Act, the prairie became the new land of opportunity, where a hardworking family could make a life, even if they had few resources other than strong backs and strong wills. "Uncle Sam is rich enough to give everyone a farm!" the people declared.

# Building a House

*You can see the dead grass in a soddy's walls.*

$\mathcal{T}$he first homesteading task was building a house. But trees for lumber were very hard to find. Only those lucky enough to have claimed land in the wooded eastern areas or along rivers and streams, where trees grew, had enough timber to build a house. Others were forced to use the prairie itself for building material. Homesteaders used oxen- or horse-drawn plows to cut up the thick mat of soil and grass called sod. The sod, held together by the dense grass roots, was cut into big slabs. Each slab was two to three feet long, four inches thick, two and a half feet wide, and weighed about fifty pounds.

*Quilts kept sleepers warm in their beds and could also serve as room dividers. During cold weather, they were hung against the walls to keep out the cold.*

*A typical soddy (facing page).*

*In this old photograph, a homestead family in Nebraska shows off their soddy built into the hillside.* THE NEBRASKA STATE HISTORICAL SOCIETY

The slabs were laid grass side down like giant, flat bricks to build sod houses, or "soddies." As he built the soddy, the homesteader left spaces for windows and a door. Mud was used to fill in any gaps and crevices between the sod slabs. The roof usually consisted of willow or cottonwood poles, crisscrossed to make a support for a layer of sod. Paper or cloth was often stretched beneath the ceiling to keep dirt from falling into the soddy from the roof. Soddies were also often built into the side of a hill, which provided part of the walls for the house and protected it from wind, rain, and the bitter cold of winter.

It took five men three weeks and ten acres of sod to build a large soddy—that's enough ground for nine football fields. Homesteaders without neighbors had to make do with a small home, often only one large room partitioned into living and sleeping areas by hanging blankets or quilts.

Sod homes could be unpleasant places to live. Mice sometimes tunneled through the sod walls, followed by snakes and other creatures not meant to live in houses. The dirt floor was uneven and hard to keep clean. But the soddy was solid and fireproof. The thick walls made it cool in summer and warm in winter. The walls could be papered with old newspapers and decorated with family pictures. Buffalo skins and rugs made from rags could help cover the floor. Over time, a successful homestead family could plaster and whitewash the inside walls and add a wooden floor.

## Starting a Farm

$O$nce the family had shelter, the next thing to be done was to begin farming. Since there was little or no money to buy supplies, and towns were far away, the majority of homestead families had to grow most of, and sometimes all, their own food. A letter from a government agent in Wyoming written in 1916 gave the following advice to a potential homesteader:

*Even though today's farmers can use machines to help with the farmwork, a few still choose to use animals, as the homesteaders did, instead of tractors.*

*A homesteader's garden was much like this modern garden, and provided crops such as squash, cucumbers, and cabbage for the family.*

*If a homesteader is on the ground ready for work by April 1st to 15th and has equipment in implements, team and feed, he can prepare a fair acreage for wheat or other small grain; if he cannot reach this, he should not fail to break land enough to plant potatoes and a variety of garden vegetables. He may, too, plant on sod without much preparation beans and peas, and be pretty sure of a crop. . . . If things to eat in sufficiency are raised the first year, the undertaking is a pronounced success and a greater growth should be made each year.*

For homesteaders, the farm work was clearly divided among the family members. The man was usually responsible for the hardest physical labor, like breaking up the prairie for planting with the help of horses or oxen. Part of the crop of corn, wheat, or other grain grown on the homestead helped feed the family. The rest was sold for cash.

The wife and children planted, weeded, and harvested the family garden. The garden grew close to the house and provided fresh vegetables and storage crops like potatoes and onions for the family. The wife or children also milked the cow and collected eggs from the chicken coop every morning. A homesteading family ate little meat. Sunday dinner was often special, for the mother of the family would slaughter a chicken, clean it, and roast it.

# Surviving on the Prairies

In the fall, the family worked hard to put aside food for the harsh winter ahead. The men and older boys harvested the grain. The women and children dug the potatoes that would help the family survive the winter. They dried fruits and vegetables, smoked and salted meat, and turned cabbage into sauerkraut.

There were no refrigerators, but for storing food each homestead had a cellar that stayed cool even during the summer because it was

*Crops such as onions, potatoes, and squash store well in cool cellars and can be used throughout the winter.*

15

underground. It had another important use. The prairie is tornado country. When a tornado threatened, the family hurried into the cellar for protection from the storm, just as prairie families do today.

Corn was a vital crop. The corn homesteaders grew was field corn, not the sweet corn we eat off the cob. The kernels of field corn are starchy rather than sweet. They can be dried and stored for months to serve as food throughout the year. Sometimes, corn was just about all there was to eat. In 1862 an article in the magazine *Nebraska Farmer* listed thirty-three ways to cook corn, including dry mush and milk, white pot (milk, eggs, cornmeal, sugar, and molasses), griddle cakes, and maize gruel for invalids.

Salt pork was another mainstay of the diet. Salt pork comes from a pig's belly, just like bacon. It consists of layers of white fat mixed with thin strips of lean meat. Salting the pork preserves it so it can be stored for long periods of time in a cool place.

The cellar could be a separate structure, used for storing food and as protection in case of a tornado.

Field corn, used for cooking and feeding livestock, dries on the plants before being harvested.

*Prairie fires spread very fast as they burn through the dry grass. Fire was perhaps the most feared danger during homesteading times.*

*Many people, including infants, died from the hardships of homesteading.*

Laura Ingalls Wilder, author of the Little House books, wrote that her mother cooked thin slices of the pork in boiling water, drained it, coated it with flour, and fried it.

Homesteaders had to count on nature to provide weather good enough to grow a year's worth of food. Prairie fires, grasshopper plagues, and droughts were just some of the threats to successful farming. Trips to town were long, difficult, and infrequent. When their crops failed, so did many homesteaders. They had to abandon their hard-won claims and head back to the cities in hope of finding another way of making a living. After the first few years of homesteading, the popular saying became, "The government bet you 160 acres of land against $18 that you will starve to death before you live on the land for five years."

## Everyday Living

*On most homesteads, the furniture was simple and handmade.*

Homesteading meant mostly hard work. In addition to the farm chores, the men had to know how to construct buildings and furniture, how to cultivate the land, how to dig a well, and how to hunt. The women sewed the family clothes, collected wild herbs and berries, and took care of the household.

Families were often large. As soon as children were old enough

*The stove was one of the few items brought to the prairie from the East.*

to help out, their mothers began to train them as workers. It was the only way the family could survive. Children learned at an early age how to make candles and soap. Young boys and girls alike helped out in the house, performing chores such as scrubbing out dirty pots with sand. Children milked cows, cleaned the barn, fed the animals, and gathered vegetables.

Homestead children also gathered buffalo chips for their prairie home. "Chips" are dried pats of manure, which were found on the prairie and used as fuel for the kitchen stove along with wood and coal. The stove was an important item in the soddy. The oven temperature was controlled by the amount and size of the pieces of fuel put in. Using their kitchen stoves, frontier women became experts at making biscuits, bread, and pies. The stove also heated the home during the winter and had a reservoir for heating water for baths and washing dishes.

Standards for cleanliness were different from those of today. Every morning, people washed their hands and faces using a pitcher and basin. Baths were a once-a-week affair in a small metal tub. Clothing was worn as long as possible between washings because doing the laundry was such a difficult chore.

In *The Price of Free Land*, Treva Adams Strait describes how her mother did the laundry on their Nebraska homestead in the early 1900s. Mr. Adams built a fireplace for heating the wash water by the nearby lake. On washday morning, Mrs. Adams and the children took the laundry by wagon to the fireplace and started a fire. While Mrs. Adams sorted the clothes, Treva and her brother Howard brought pails of water to fill half of the big metal boiler placed on the fireplace. When the water came to a boil, Mrs. Adams added soap shavings and stirred until the soap dissolved. She dumped in the white clothes, boiled them for ten minutes, then removed the heavy, steaming clothing with a broomstick. She rubbed any remaining stains with soap, then scrubbed them out on a ribbed washboard. After removing the white clothes, Mrs. Adams added colored ones to the boiling water. After those she washed the heavy work clothes. Last, she dipped the water out with a bucket and filled the boiler with fresh rinse water.

While Mrs. Adams did the wash, Treva and Howard gathered driftwood from the shores of the lake for the fire. The wet laundry was loaded onto the wagon and brought back to the house. Then

*This young child is learning to shell peas, a chore that is easy to learn. Just like this mother, homestead mothers also taught their young children simple chores so they could help out as soon as possible.*

*Even in below-freezing winters, homesteaders had to use an outside bathroom or "outhouse."*

each item had to be hung out to dry. The exhausting work of doing the laundry could take up the entire day, leaving little time for anything else. It wasn't uncommon for a woman to stand on one foot while doing the laundry, using the other foot to rock a baby's cradle.

As homestead children grew older, the boys worked more outside, helping their fathers in the fields, while girls continued to help care for the youngest children and learn household tasks such as sewing, an especially important skill for them to master.

*Using this basic equipment, homestead women spent all day scrubbing clothes clean one piece at a time.*

*Stores were few and far between and could only stock a small selection during homesteading times, so many people ordered from the Sears Roebuck catalogue, which sold all sorts of items by mail, from plows to dishes to clothing.*

Ready-made clothing was expensive, so most families made their own clothes. They wasted nothing, saving the bits of leftover fabric to use in making quilts. Sewing, and especially quilting, became social activities, and frontier women developed great skill at creating designs from bits of fabric. Women would gather to make special quilts celebrating important occasions, such as a new preacher coming to town or a wedding. Such traditions continue today.

*Quilting is a time-consuming activity for Marsha Dunn, as it was for homestead women (above).*

*Quilts often have special meanings. Each square in this modern quilt, stitched by Marsha Dunn, was made by a different child and represents things important to him or her.*

# Prairie Schools

$\mathcal{G}$etting an education was difficult during the homestead era. In the early days, classes were held in homes and churches when there wasn't money to build a school. At first, families had to pay to send their children to school, which was difficult for many. A typical fee for a four-month term was $1.00 to $1.50 per child—the price of a pair of children's shoes—a luxury for some homestead families. English was not the native language for many immigrant children, so school was hard for them. Classes were often held only during the cold winter months or the summer. Children were needed at home as workers during spring planting and fall harvesting.

*A one-room school during homesteading times.*
Denver Public Library

*This old one-room schoolhouse served homestead children (facing page).*

25

*Some rural areas are still served by one-room schools like Valley View School in northwestern Montana (right).*

*This old school is empty now, but the desks from the days when it was used remain (below).*

Most children did not attend school past the eighth grade. The high schools were in the towns, too far away for country children to travel to every day. Sending a child to high school meant not only paying room and board to a town family, but losing a valuable worker, as well.

The homestead children got up between 4 and 5 A.M. to do their chores before walking to school, often miles away. During the winter they were lucky to get home before dark. Most country schools had few students, all taught in one room by the same teacher. The teachers were men or single women; married women were not allowed to teach school. The teachers were often only teenagers and did not necessarily have much training.

Today, hundreds of children still attend country schools. When the eighteen children in grades one through five arrive in the morning at Valley View School in northwestern Montana, they hang their coats in the mudroom and go into the classroom, where their desks are arranged in a circle. Just as in any other modern American school, the walls are decorated with student projects. An assortment of books lines the shelves. Central heating keeps the school comfortably warm, and a student teacher helps teach the children.

The old-time country school was a simpler place. A stove in the center heated the room unevenly. Each child brought his or her lunch in a bucket, along with a cup for drinking well water. When Howard Adams went off to school the first time, his mother put peanut butter and jelly sandwiches, an apple, and homemade cookies in his bucket. Each child also brought along a slate, which was like a miniature blackboard, and a piece of chalk to write on the slate. After an assignment was finished and checked by the teacher, the child could erase the slate and use it again for the next assignment.

Desks or tables were arranged in rows so the students faced the teacher. The students learned basic skills—reading, writing, and arithmetic. They didn't have much opportunity for creative projects. There were few books besides basic textbooks. Few schools even had reference materials such as a dictionary, an atlas, and a globe.

*Many homestead children learned reading skills from books like* The Primer, *a 1910 school reader featuring folktales.*

# Having Fun

The hardest-working people also know how to have fun. In homesteading times, people entertained themselves mostly by doing things together. Music was an important part of many homestead families' lives. Like many men, Laura Ingalls Wilder's father played the fiddle on cold winter evenings while the family sang along to his tunes. Many families saved up money to buy a piano or a small organ. Reading together by the warmth and light of the fire was another way of enjoying the evening, even though the Bible and perhaps an almanac were the only reading materials for many families.

Children often made their own toys. Girls sewed homemade dolls and made clothes for them, while boys whittled toys from wood scraps.

And of course, the outdoors offered many chances for exploration and play. Hide-and-seek, swimming, and picnics provided summertime fun, while sliding down snowy hills and building snowmen kept the children busy in the wintertime.

Life may have been difficult in many ways for homestead children, but they knew how to enjoy themselves and had the satisfaction of knowing they were helping to build a future for themselves and their families.

*Music played an important role in family life on the homestead.*

*Today, as in homesteading times, children have fun inventing outdoor games using only what nature and the prairie provide (facing page).*

29

# Afterword

*O*espite the offer of free land, homesteading didn't become popular until after the Civil War ended, in 1865. The war left many people homeless, ready to start a new life in a new place. Special rules made it easy for Union Army veterans to homestead, and newly freed slaves were eager to make homes for themselves and their families. A new wave of European immigrants also came to the new frontier.

In 1913, homestead claims peaked. Railroads and the telegraph had made transportation and communication easier. Inventors developed farm machinery that required less human and animal energy. Breeders came up with new varieties of grain that needed less water and produced larger crops. These advances, along with new government laws that made it easier to prove up, allowed over 53 percent of homesteaders to do so by the turn of the century. Before 1900, fewer than 30 percent of homesteaders proved up.

As late as 1936, a few homestead claims were still being filed. It wasn't until 1976, more than a hundred years after Lincoln signed the Homestead Act, that Congress passed laws making homesteading a thing of the past. The goal of the act had been accomplished. After taking the land from American Indians and forcing them to leave, the government had transferred more than 270 million acres to private ownership, greater than 10 percent of the total area of the United States. The backbreaking work of the homesteaders has resulted in one of the most productive agricultural regions in the world today.

*The Great Northern Railroad, which went across North Dakota and Montana, brought many homesteaders to their land and provided them with vital supplies (facing page).*

# Index